Conversational Topography

From Me to You

Macheté

Copyright © 2016 by *Macheté*

De la Noche Publications:

DELANOCHEARTS@OUTLOOK.COM

First Printing, April 2016

ISBN-13: 978-0692698501
ISBN-10: 0692698507

De la Noche Publications and *Macheté* are the property of Tres Amigos.

Printed in America!

To: **Me...**

...partially freeing my heart

Let the games begin...

Table of contents:

Mauriceology

Forecasting Poetically

Endocrine glands 92

For *my* loved ones:

More than "thank you" or "gracias", is what I will say. Without the concrete, humane support from you, I wouldn't have been allowed to live in my own world, which brings my abstract, and, in itself, heartfelt style of communication to fruition. I am almost as crazy as daytime hours allow and not many people want to be around that, which I surely have no problem with. I am me.

Grandma- Dearly and serenely from everywhere in my heart, I love you. I feel your warm energy from Heaven and I see that smile. All your blessings to me I use to procure a warm place in my heart, causing me to breathe easy. You bore my mother; she bore me...here I am! You help me through all of my days and nights- but it's up to me to make life right with your help. Each time the sun shines on me I think of you and opportunity; who and what else could it be? I wish I knew how to utilize your strength in my world, maybe today is a start? Save me a plate of those dishes you cook every day in your branch of Heaven.

Grandma Helen- Your watchful eye is watching me. I must say I love you as well. I know I talked your ears off until I said " bye Grandma Helen." I made sure you knew my voice about life and I know it stuck with you. Your added blessings give me a smile because both of my grandmothers are smiling at me from heaven.

Momma: Where do I start? Not enough space for me to write about you. As the reason I have life as a canvas, you gave me my heart and voice- an infinite gift. Every trial and tribulation you saw me through: open opinionating, intellectual self-esteem, and outspokenness- all came from you. My craziness? I will never know where that came from, aren't we still trying to figure that out? You are the only human who always has no problem telling me the truth about myself, plain. I appreciate the life you gave me and the love you applied to me, we both know I need it. I honor you as my mother- you know I'll be crazy for the rest of my life. I love you. Cheers!!!

Marlo: My not so little brother. We have had a wild lifestyle for its entirety, and you surely know what type of brother you have. I'm glad you grew up faster than me to a certain extent because it gives me something to be proud of. When we were young teenagers, you showed me aspects of the streets that people twice our age couldn't. Shall I say we have resilience? I shall, I shall. Thank you for bringing me a nephew...that's my best friend. My time will come.

Daddy- The old man. I thank you for being in my life and having a presence. I learned to play tennis through you without tennis lessons. You showed me how to recognize elders and to never forget that all I'll ever have in this life is my brother and mother. As your eldest son, I wonder if you know why I'm so crazy? Ask Uncle Dayrll what he thinks about me being crazy? He cusses like a sailor! Besides me, he's the craziest dude ever: cutt-off shorts and knee high socks, no t-shirt in Chickasaw Park. I miss the 90's.

Myron: My beautiful nephew. I owe you for making me happy every day. You are my best friend. During the lowest and rather recent parts of my life, you were the only human to help me out of my low times and you are only three years old. When I was sad on the couch, every morning I heard you wake up and say "Maurice, where's Maurice?" Then I'd hear you jump off the bed, so I'd go hide, you'd come looking for me and say "Maurice...Maurice...oh Mauriiiice...Maurice!" When you started getting mad because you couldn't find me, I'd come out of hiding because it was so funny that I couldn't hold it in. Thank you forever my 'lil dude, my 'lil man. Young King.

Fin

Introduction:

Conversational Topography is a lifestyle I created to encompass all aspects of communication in my life, such as reading and writing, and utilize them to build from the bottom but most pertinent level of socialization or interaction, which is verbal or sign, by using a topographical format- essentially a topographic map to convey the many different heights that normal conversations can reach. Take the experiences you have in life and build from them. The poems in this collection sing various songs about life: friends turn enemies, false representatives of the state (haha), lost loved ones, inaccuracies in life, joy, death, being alive, and many more. If you enjoy reading true words about true stories that convey life as an art form, you may enjoy reading this collection. These poems stem from the bottom of my heart and nowhere else, while representing the pains I have in my life that I have to get off of my chest before they consume me. While this first volume of topography spreads its foundation, another volume of original topography is close to completion...look for it soon. Enjoy the art of my conversation if you can, at least try to, that is all I ask.

About the author

I must etch myself somewhere in print and stone, so first I aim to free the pains in my heart by presenting raw form poetry to whatever audience I have. I'll do something else later to etch myself in stone.

What I mean by "raw form poetry" is poetry that has no traditional barriers and is free of criticism from stiffs because a stiff cannot be human, it can only drink from a bottomless cup and continue to deny your self-expression. I have no barriers in my life and I like to express myself without being told what to do, unless it's from a superior power. Even then I'm like "arggggh!" Slap me.

My sentiments toward self-expression are what allowed me the right angle to showcase my introductory poetry gallery to poetry lovers and potential readers. For now, let my work speak for me...tell me what you think.

Conversational Topography

From Me to You

Macheté

Short but potently crisp

Me 2007, 2

This year I've learned again,
I've grown in how I live.
A better way to make money,
a new way to keep a friend.
A solid way to form a bond and
never lose that friend,
what to do
in event that friend gives in;
when the money falls short
or if the world nears end.

A-New

A must be for me is a very clear thought,
handy like a back-up plan with no flaws.
Much needed like a shower
to wash the dirt off.

Bafoonery

Some adults need to be in elementary school,
with children of their own they seem to be lost.
Forgetting the fact that this
world is for luring you into a trap,
regardless of costs.

3 minutes

With very little time in complicated rhyme,
I pose cold truth in pixelated kind.
Fuck the middle man I want the main man,
quiet at my post, dodging hurtful hands.

1989

I saw a picture recently from 1989,
four years old and my brother on my side.
New and playdough- he was one at the time,
we look not guilty
but now that's a lie.

Untitled

Being "black"
you have no starting place,
you just
jump into things,
hoping to pave the way.

What the fuck

The efforts I exert in forms of rhyme and reason
mean nothing to the perp that has no mean to reason.
The people of today who work inside of names
cannot give chance to help many advance,
instead they surely give it all to the hand.

Silent words

Most people I see stroll just as the rest,
matching dress and talk
seemingly born abreast.
I daily note most move
while very few maneuver,
harmless are the ones that move
because they seek no suture.
Feared and hated are the few
maneuvering to suture.

Me 2007

In any case I man up,
like watching ass fest on an eighty-five inch;
eye tight I am with my own accent.

With no help I stand erect
like a mad stray during a pillage.
I am to kill he who enters my village,
looking to,
take from me or change how I'm living.

Crazy thoughts

Have you
seen someone,
who can't look human?
Body normal shape but features not congruent?
Ears twitch when speaking, eyes do the same-
almost like a maze that picks your brain.
Sickly in their nature,
they only learn how
to interact with nature without gettin' sunburnt-
from those who came before they saw earth.

Poetry

Mentally flinching is written on paper,
etched by sticks, emitting sweet vapors.
Frugal wordplay is the object of this,
letters turn words that build ant hills
stark on darts at poetry gent,
not blowing steam based on circumference,
never for writing misleading content,
always at risk to keep readers drawn in.

Mensajes

Correctamente yo respondo
a muchos mensajes,
a veces no digo nada
porque no necesito.
Mi atención es para
mi computacion,
no para otras personas
quien mira para los cómicos.
Yo sé mucho sobre las personas,
y yo estoy contento con Uds.-
porque muchas personas
quiere nada de vida.
¿Pero yo?
Yo quiero muy mucho de vida.

Mauricio

Mensajes, English translation

Messages

Correctly I respond
to many messages,
sometimes I say nothing
because I don't need.
My attention is for
my computation,
not for other people
who look for the comics.
I know much about the people
and I am content with them,
because many people
want nothing from life.
But me?
I want much from life.

Precursors on the brinks

Compromises

No door will open if no deal is made,
one is the loser the other will profit,
nothing is sure by a spin of the bottle,
luck of the draw or picking of straws.
To make the right deal, third parties are off,
just two in the circle creating the laws.
Man and woman must surely agree
on places for planting and harvesting seeds.

Prime Meridian

Mother nature is awaken when I wake up,
she sends spies for me deep into the rough,
knowing I'm trouble for most around me,
not 'cause I'm bad but 'cause what I scream-
Life!
Life!
Humanely serious,
my eyes watch the land get devoured by the sick,
unhealthy and sad with a European grip!
The healthy fall back to let mother nature deal,
father went north but almost got killed-
now,
I hear all the cries turn shrill.

Mother nature knows me, I look close to she,
can hear what she hears, can see what she sees.

Just, far down there

Lookin' down from my cliff I saw something move,
scoping my eyes to analyze it,
adjusting my sight, this can't be true-
I see myself looking back at me!
My heart beats with utter buoyancy,
how in the hell did I get down there?
Thinking twice out loud...is *Macheté* here?
He is who I'm looking at down there?
I swear to myself I threw him away,
slit both wrists to drain my veins
of poisonous thoughts *Macheté* relays
as arrows of power surrounded by flames!
A part of me that I never show thee,
it's been ten years, I still sense evil
dark on the eyes of his rojo pupil,
he might have changed but I feel his lethal,
ready for me to begin his sequel.
Way up here I hear deep breathing,
clouds are forming, I smell the reefer,
dawn is not close, I sense the release
of interatomic bionic kinesis-
barriers broke, *Macheté* is breaching!
Floating his way from a few thousand deep-
up to my cliff, within two feet,
growling at me without showing teeth,
snaking intent to rattle on me
if I don't place him back in the streets.

Looking at him, I say to him:

"drink and smoke, love the women,
before daylight, you better be in..."

Red Ink

The tables are turning in permanent ways,
those who had houses turn into strays-
strays that suffered are taking a stand,
armed with intent to leave blood on the land,
sick of no aid from economic pains,
militant strays are formed every day.
Laced with fire to feed a family,
humans like this are not for candy,
nor qualify for humanitarian-
surely will make it through an Armageddon.
Many will suffer from having thin skin,
en route to the sun may the have nots win.

Bafoonery, 2

As I migrate to work
swerving through traffic,
induced by green,
I see many things,
cars trailing cars-
don't take open lanes,
modern day slaves.
Wrecks happen often and
people wonder why,
they had plenty space but
chose to trail behind.
These people had choice,
instead chose to die.

Who is the culprit

Walking through my day I felt the rain,
almost like hail, same strength anyway-
soon I realized it was salt in the sky,
shook my dreads out and ran to a close tree,
began to think- *why is salt chasing me,*
real deal salt to disintegrate me?
Other people walking had sun on them,
maybe even rain, no one had salt.
I look in my mind and question grandma-
in truth,
help me find who threw salt.

Uncle Thomasina, fuckin' slave

Thou must be weak to try the game,
like a referee they report everything-
those against the grain, those who free think,
even telling fibs to inflate wrong things,
down with uncle Sam who takes and takes,
against momma Joe with staff in her leg,
push her down steps just to gain a half step
in off-road world where few percent twirl,
avid at blocking the truth in the swirl,
hiding in sight in the blank man's world.

Uncle Scrooge

How dare you break up a family affair,
mad at your age and the falling of hair
straight from the scalp of a barren old man-
if married- misery- if not, misery.
At polls stand strong around us stand weak,
many hurt hearts will catch you in the streets,
work you on hellidays for a small fee-
we didn't do it your government did,
tenure plus hate can do nothing for you,
broke with no escape, you are Uncle Scrooge!

El Invierno

Hoy es hace frio!
¿Dónde está mi pistola?
Necesito más calor
porque gentes estan muy loco,
creen que estan importante,
actualmente estan nada.
Yo monto a bicicleta grande
cubir más terreno,
yo siempre mira para oro
construir mi imperio.
Nadie es terminando mis aventuras,
estoy el chairman del baja mundo!

Hoy es hace frio!
¿Dónde está mi pistola?
La fecha es ahora,
para construiendo mi mundo,
entonces mi vida,
entonces mi imperio.
A veces yo siento muy preocupado
porque yo vivo un poco peligroso.

El Invierno, English translation

The Winter

It's cold today!
Where is my pistol?
I need more heat
because people are very crazy.
They think they are important,
actually they are nothing.
I ride a big bike
to cover more terrain,
I always look for gold
to construct my empire.
Nobody is terminating my adventures,
I am the chairman of the underworld.

It's cold today!
Where is my pistol?
The time is now
to construct my world,
then my life,
then my empire.
Sometimes I am very worried
because I live a little dangerous...

Clash of the titans

It who spawned first gave way to second-
second is younger, weaker, unruly,
first reigns king of knowledge and blessing,
able to lace loose stringing of second.

As second grows age it learns to grace,
first is on looking with powerful grins,
knowing that second is destined to change,
going for the best, maybe for a win.

Second has no leeway to see that far,
seldom calls first by title not name,
until one day, first gave him a scar,
second grew grief and called first a bad name.

First heaved a hook that made the ground split,
out came a puzzle of parts that might fit
if second is found in good health and sound-
now all is lost until they meet ground.

Tom Ebenezer

Stingy, careless, doubtful, scary-
knowing you are wrong,
but yet you don't care,
living your days by that book in your hand.

What's sad about you
is you have a heart too,
never is it shown unless to your own,
endless benefits, yet you itemize?
Must have a receipt for all that you buy.

Stingy, careless, doubtful, scary-
everyone is gone,
no loved ones to bury,
money is *nothing* compared to a family.

Now you all alone around the hellidays,
this is what you wanted, got what you paid.
Soulless as you are real tears still fall
down your stone cold face, hurt and alone.

Catch Phrases

The sun is my gold
in ray form not ore,
a few light years
before I was born,
someone was me-
full of ancient scripts.
A raw form of me
hovers as a blimp,
looking over seas
to park my spaceship.

The stars are my eyes,
I see everywhere-
moving as a tide
to quietly stare
into dark minds
of souls out there-
out there as guides
to stork for the bare.

The moon is my boost-
if the lights go out
I look to the moon
and climb my way out.

Randomness

Dire straights

At the age of 29 I refine my mind,
even let the other two in my cage out.
I have no choice, henceforth I form a pact
to never let a weak person stab me in the back.

I have been too nice in ways I will never be
to many ugly people who cannot look at me.

At the age of 29 I refine my mind,
to go for the gold I dispose of fake souls,
and all the ugly people that I use to know,
these people want nothing
are bumps in the road.

A sad Life

Color is not the reason we suffer,
ignorance of law would be that reason.
Think about the real, the media kills,
you see a rich black, that there is a buffer,
behind the scenes these people are blubber
sold for a dollar less than a quarter.
Don't sign contracts unless you wrote 'em,
drinking the sexy truth is the magic potion.
They shot 'ya boy because he couldn't hold it in,
Hola! to Assata, dreadlocks in the wind!
Grown men speak their mind,
little guys stay in line,
a few of us study a few of us shine.
Saving everyone just cannot be done...
more than a few get to walk in the sun.

Off in the woodies

A brick cabin with three or four rooms,
double in story, perfect honeymoon.
Next to a grove of fruits and greens,
not far from water, enclosed by tress.
Mother nature walks by,
cracks a smile and walks off,
thinking the cabin is home to a ghost.
If she knew only what brewed inside!
Teams of Firestarters occupying every room,
with superglue-
the plan is wrapped by just a few.
This cabin is a small home front for the future...

not far from water, enclosed by trees.

Small thing sharp brain

An itty bitty guy small like a French fry,
blessed with a heart in the art of disguise.
Eyes with doorways to that pineal,
brownish red skin has the hint of melanin-
the first four lines are a small palm print
of a complex man en route to call wind.
It will not be fair but nothing really is,
no need to sit with a heart this big.
An itty bitty guy swinging hard like a giant
is the first to rob, the first to quit quiet.
Humans like this don't cry out in vain,
centuries of hate are buried by fate.

Body language expert

Without a word said or any motor play
the body walks a deep lane of its current state.
Emitted through pores as uncut terms,
a language expert can arrange quiet words.

Quicker than an eye blink
your stance is understood,
intentions are noted as bad or good.
Years of living,
blended with instinctive learning,
graduates a full body language expert
from normal thought that only mouths can talk,
to truth of knowing that *every body talks*.

Response; Circling the sun

My energy shifts from that of a serf
to that of a king who has peace on this earth.
When stars grow it may show on my face,
when I lash out have I fallen from grace?

I think to myself as I question myself,
maybe I have too much time to myself?
A minor in height but veteran in thought,
and strength,
is through written word how I vent?
Is fault in my verse?
If so to what extent?

Why would you go last?

Momma fixed our plates first,
I said "why you go last?"
A question as a statement,
got my point across fast.
She said she didn't know,
had a glow on her head,
"that's how she is"
is what my brother said-
of course his boy of two jibbed in...
"granny, granny, where's mine at..."
I love all the moments
that we all share,
so far in life
momma always been there.
Takes care of us first,
then she goes last.

Free form poetry

Absent of all rules, valiant type writing
free from traditional scale and lighting
excluding the rules of English 101
including a form of uneven gun shots
the reader can follow if broken from rule
open to free words teachers ridicule
subtracting non-troves of things in school
adding gems of spice I gained in strife
equals me now, a prowler for life

Questions

More often than not I question myself,
shall I be me and utilize stealth?
Or shall I be weak, short myself to an elf?
Who am I to me? How am I perceived?

More often than not I question myself,
did school help me, did I help myself?
The pressure is cooking, what is really boiling?
It was out all night but did it really spoil?

Is
it ok,
that
at my age I can barely think straight?
Like when boy meets girl,
everything changes.

Mirando a mi vida

In deep thought I'm interplanetary,
walking through portals, no gravity laws.
In pure spirit form, resembling a prism,
found on every street of the ten dimensions.
Using algebra, I engage in chemistry
almost in mid-air, floating with grace.
Mixing dark matter from the deepest of black
into a substance, once applied it won't crack.
Crafting my body from feet to head,
a human is free and bound to the land.

Soul Sentiments

A few years ago

At night,
I used to curl up in my bed.
Not because I'm grimey,
not because I'm sorry,
but because-
how the family did my grandma!
Sold the house kept the money,
put her in a nursing home
on a dirty 'ole cot,
they just let her rot.

Leaves of grass

Reach back many thousands to
acknowledge the truth,
once you gain your conscious
no one can stop you.

In light of the struggle
the dream team will lose,
in the complex puzzle
alive is the truth.

Retain what you study
to form what you feel,
indulge in your culture
so you they won't steal.

What gives?

Since I'm young
older folk talk down on me,

since I'm me,
the white folk frown at me.
Before I was broke
people could find me,
now that I'm broke,
no one can find me-
damn!
Are they lookin' for me?
Since I've been broke,
the wealthy point and laugh at me,
what gives?

Family is so weak...

Only in event of a major hurricane,
family comes around mad strong when it rains.
If nobody dies, if nobody wins
the big ticketed lottery, nobody cares.
Matriarchs wear a crown of the shell,
once she moves on that great shell melts.
A weakening family cared not to build,
sought keeping up with hands on the fiddle.
Forgot what they had in their hands was the truth,
lost old jewels pertinent to use
in new school ways from old school rules.
Under your pillow the following truth,
yes,
not a quarter, forget a green dollar-
'tis the last note of your family's mother:

"Honor my love, I loved your lives,
you forgot me since I went to the sky."

Feel that...

Untitled, 2

In good spirit,
I,
smile more than I cry,
walking on the edge of a brittle mountain top
with a heartbeat of pure gold blood
I see the wind and I see the sun.
Life is of sun that livens my shadow,
even when I'm low inside, I smile.

In good spirit,
I,
smile more than I cry,
depression is coded as long term pressure.
A broke day now then a rich day next,
capture a shot of something that matters and
never forget what you saw made you smile.

In good spirit,
I,
smile more than I cry.

I am everything you can't think of

A blank metaphor for the bones of a skull,
I remain me, I'll never sell my soul.
May fight may cuss may shoot may vice,
expressing to admit I've done dirt all my life.
Please don't think I cheat for mine,
in line,
I stand while many sit down.
Stare at me and frown or frown at me and frown
with utter discontent like staring at rain clouds-
searching for sun while the sky is falling down,
time for a meteor so I can get down.

I've been dead until now

I've been dead until now,
wiping a brow steeped in sweat
with a weak wrist,
gelling within.
Stress eats me through a breached mainframe,
using me to clone a weak boned man-
hurt from more than being beat down.

Sunny days turn cloudy and chances
of rain on my parade are one-hundred percent,
deep within,
I know this struggle is meant...

I smile 'cause I'm alive and
surely frown 'cause I'm hurt-
seen a female in a skirt built
like she's from the dirt,
seen an old couple stroll, the
old man tipped his hat-
my tenseness left, I smiled and waved back.

When I was dead,
I felt like T.V. in 1940,
while other people in the struggle
lived in color-
deep within,
I know this struggle is meant...

hurting my heart without my consent,
weakening beats that pump my blood-
I might dry out without some love.

Until now I've been dead,
but no one could tell.
A few months ago my heartbeat fell,
alive for some reason? 'Cause I'm alive,
my blood went cold within my mind.

I've been dead until now.

Sometimes

What lies inches away
seems too far to reach,
like a white t-shirt
that's too hard to bleach.
If someone you love
is too far to reach,
do you stand at the corner
alone and obsolete?
Or do you take the risk
and walk across the street?

Comparisons

The grass was greener yesterday than it is today,
      sun was so much brighter,
      water tasted better,
food was healthier and that caused it to be pleasant.
      Everything was lovely,
      everyone was lively,
never did a time occur that people were not vibing.
      Socially enlightening,
      singles became married.
Hearts opened doors they may never close.

Many women

Who told Argo to beat you?
This man is not your mother,
a gem like you
should be treated much better.
Scratches,
scars,
swelling and pain
drown your soft face as you walk through the rain.
Who told Argo to beat you?
Sittin' black eyed as you fix your hair,
miss lady I'm sorry,
this mirror does not lie.
That blood is real,
those tears that you secrete
are Moses as a stream that parts the Red Sea-
falling from your face then onto the floor,
slowing you down as you fix for the day.
Who told Argo to beat you?

From Me to you

The future will hold the pressure to live,
some take note of the power within.
A moment to spare is a moment to lose,
if you need help take cover and shoot.
Timing and planning are needed to win,
the longer you fight the more they give in.
This kingdom is yours provided by light,
sources are here to use in your life...

Grow crops, grow trees, bear fruit, kill weeds-
rid of trash the way dentist's clean teeth.
Don't host those who don't help life,
things uproar in the heat of night.
From me to you I am speaking my peace,
the meeting for truth will be in the street!

Self-named greed doesn't care if you eat,
from me to you I am speaking my peace.

How I feel

At this moment I'm slower than normal,
still upbeat but rather informal.
I cannot be me if I'm tied up with them,
I cannot be me if I'm not who I am.
Demeaning to me is my hourly pay,
an platonic boost would ease my day.

Thoughts are an eagle so therefore I fly,
soon as I fly I fall to the ground-
the air is polluted, I do not know how
to seed a good living without going wild,
it's not my choice, I do not know how.
Alone how I stand and stable my aim,
the losses I take I charge to the game.
Resorting to chaos is seeming the choice,
love inside me is losing its voice.

Rare form

Please know
all day,
men fall to women,
to argue is slow,
what men bare children?

Respect mothers' mind,
and she of steel who
is soft to the touch
to control how you feel.

As man,
gain wealth,
ensure through the winter,
prevent each foot
from meeting the splinter.

As man,
take pride in wearing your crown,
if times grow bare you can't lose ground.

Joven

Where ever did you go?
What if I never know?
Time and time I think
this girl ain't comin' back-
time and time I think-
what will it take for me
to show you that I'm sorry
and just what you mean to me?
I wish that you come back,
let me speak my peace!
I haven't felt the same since
you left me in the deep,
deep cold snow-
with *no way* to reach Joven...

...

Mauriceology

¿Gavilla o no gavilla?

No gavilla para me,
porque gavillas del Americanas
no tienen manos de guerra,
pero tienen manos de television,
y quieren manos de actor y actrices.
Asi no gavilla para me!

¿Gavilla o no Gavilla? Translation

Gang or no Gang?

No gang for me
because American gangs
don't have hands of war
but have hands of television,
and hands of actors and actresses.
So, no gang for me.

The population of me

DNA wrapped tight,
genome of truth,

RNA got loose,
soon fell right back,
no more relapse.

Blood flows as heat
through veins of snow,
straight to the brain,
light to the show.

Bridge me baby

Away from ethics and morals
into mischief and quarrels,
a brief time resting
in the quest moving forward.
Free lunch is not given
even if you're street ridden,
right now I'm not
still nothin' has been given.

Life is hard for me,
but when I wake up-
I may look sad but I'm alive so I'm nigh.
Vigilant,
the Lynch ideal makes me sick,
tearing up quick makes my teeth grit.
Less forty's mule
I'm winning with this losing hand,
if Afri can then *Ameri* can.

De la Noche, *my disclaimer*

Don't crucify me,
I am not to blame.
I know it's very easy
to relocate your shame,
everyday your summer
includes a winter rain.

Don't crucify me,
I never play to maim,
my heart is on my sleeve
but this pistol's on my waist!
What trickled down to me
is that my grandmother gave-
time and time again
but was treated as a slave
by her braindead family-
take my words to the grave!

Don't crucify me,
not hard to feel my vibe,
as the truth cloaks me
pain inundates my eyes.
Don't crucify me,
because you lost your touch?
I kneel by a palm tree and
manufacture a Dutch
to settle my tummy
before I throw up!
Sanding down my soul-
for how they did grandma
haunts me til' I'm old

now I have a deep cough.

Don't crucify me!

Macheté

My domain

In the mist of my pain I shower in the rain
to wash away failure, then try life again.
My domain is earth but seldom am I here,
whenever I return, I notice everywhere
that people never change so never do I care.
Changing for the better is a natural affair
that most people lack like knowledge of self.
I am me forever, as long as I can see,
no need to wish me well-
the heavens watch me.

Outside

I frolic as father nature,
no shirt no pants!
Trying to impress mother nature if I can.

Amino Acids

Poetry and law, that's about it-
mastering these avoids a fall,
forming a wall not many could scale,
verbally steep, griot not frail.

Poetry and law, that's about it,
what to learn but laws of Earth?
Paving paths of national words
grown by tongue or by pen.

Poetry and law, that's about it,
knowing a little is better than none,
if all else fails do not miss this-
poetry and law, that's about it!

Deceptive throw, Deviant catch

Collecting much data to use for later,
racing in my sneakers, dodging the snakes.
Isolating self just for self-gateway,
moving at a rate without much trace-
infiltrating me would need mother nature,
nuclei of genius have made my clay
away from bad corn, close to my nature;
leaving out weeds that obscure concentration.

Every single time

Parked like a narc was he of jealousy,
full of ill will because he is lacking.
Short of the muscle it takes to bring smiles-
too small to meet eyes he looks at the ground.
Not man enough to speak up about truth,
hidden are feelings he hopes to come true.
Stepping on toes of his fellow classmates,
to reach his goal he will do all it takes.
Toying with money that people will need,
pocketing quick with ill-gotten proceeds,
paying his taxes to shadow elite-
whatever is left he must keep discreet.

You look like, but aren't us.

No wonder you have no shadow,
you look but speak like them.
Your claims to help the helpless
are words to block the ears
of those who listen closely
to those who oil the gears.
To quell the mouth of question
and those of no fear,
you promise an answer
and you preach of love and jeer.

A sound from other races
is not for us to hear,
but now the speech to help was built
from words you learned from them?
Unnatural paternal
is sewn from secret pixels,
in terms of wealth and power
you hold for ten percent.
You look much like us
but you speak just like them.

Straight

I tell it to your face, no not to forgive,
for those who moved, there's time to repent.
Without sharing truth all we see is a fool,
a house nigger smiling for those it salutes,
portraying a person who claims to have power-
away from the scene you lay flat on your back
and chant so much death your soul is devoured,
paid for your time, so money don't matter.
"Kill em" they scream, and smiling while said,
a long term goal is to see us all dead.

An expressive person

On my terrain
I am
very loud
like a grin,
my cup is too full
I cannot hold it in!
Around me is nothing-
just my three personas,
we laugh joke and cry,
never are we phony.
Not afraid to speak,
not afraid to stand,
not afraid to wield
the power in my hands.
All I have is me so
fuck helping them,
my cup is too full
I cannot hold it in!

Blaims and claims

Is it my fault of theirs?
His fault or hers?
Something is causing my insides to burn.
Not nature nor god would lay this on me,
something is causing my insides to weep.

The sheeple are present and ever so meager,
I am not them and I will not be weaker.

Fault me if by blood I fight,
I clear out the vault then run to the light.
Few souls are here, together we build,
always take note of the power within.

Off the top

¿Como esta joven?
Yo soy el rey, en entrenando,
llámame peligroso.
¡Mi nombre es *Macheté*!
¿Dónde está Mauricio?
¿En su edificio?
Dígale que yo dije ¡Hola!
¿Qué estás haciendo
con este gran cerebro?
¿Nada es que lo dice?
Entonces yo digo esto,
mírame empezar a monarca,
quien no puede sentir eso?
Hasta yo tengo eso gran cerebro,
yo hago nada, yo hago nada-
porque mi cerebro
es muy, muy pequeño!

I tried...

Off the top, English translation:

How are you young lady?
I am a king in training,
call me dangerous.
My name is Macheté!
Where is Mauricio?
En his building?
Tell him I said Hola!
What are you doing
with this big brain?
Nothing is what you say?
Then I say this,
watch me build a monarch,
who cannot feel that?
Until I have that big brain-
I do nothing...I do nothing...
because my brain
is very, very small.

Lying to live

Denying the truth is regarded as cruel,
why live a lie that would taint your construal?
When nothing is needed to brighten the fool,
denying the truth is regarded as cruel.

Why live a lie that would taint your construal?
The joker just said this joke is on you,
denying the truth is regarded as cruel.
Why live a lie that would taint your construal?

At night when you wash you can't soap the truth,
denying the truth is regarded as cruel.
Why live a lie that would taint your construal?
Acknowledge your presence to sharpen your tool.

Denying the truth is regarded as cruel,
why live a lie that would taint your construal?
Portraying an image of question and gloom,
denying the truth is regarded as cruel.

Why live a lie that would taint your construal?
Know who you are to be one of the few,
denying the truth is regarded as cruel.
Why live a lie that would taint your construal?

Forecasting Poetically

All

No congruency,
no fluency,
no counter mind,
all tyranny.

No open ear,
all closed heart,
no real care,
all play card.

No good future,
all bad tutor,
all clone being,
all clone speech.

All the same fate,
all size or rank,
all the same dirt,
all the same date.

Poetry, 2

Shall I change who I am to create dull grins?
Questions for the cell base of my audience.
Bring a bouquet of the darkest flower scent and
leave it in the middle of a human flower bed-
leaving me with choices, should I pick the best?
Should I pick a summer breeze and a sugar wind?
Or a winter wind with the coldest pine trees
that never can dull any moment in my schemes?

Questions for the cell base of my audience,
leave me a comment for this argument:
People are just what you think of them as,
business isn't pleasure if you say they can.
Questions for the cell base of my audience,
what's more important, looks or life skills?
Flowers that don't wilt, or flowers that will?
Hold on...
how many petals don't wilt?
Place it in the freezer and watch it won't,
my answer is a winter wind with the coldest trees.

Eye

I'm a ticking time bomb in human form-
sometimes I go off like firework shows,
other times uniform like a quiet storm,
where I go next is what I don't know.
Pitching the plan only creates catchers
and I don't need catchers, I keep my skin,
mostly no shedding in true form I am.
Tossing out the bone to have them fetch,
some of them shine but under contract;
whenever that ends they all dry out,
what's left is only a knife in their backs.
Loud apologies we hear from their mouths,
never have they spoken to us as souls
but only as peasants who have no place.
For who chose that- I feel no sorrow,
those who grew with me will feel the same.

Interchangeable options

Hobbies of mine can be hobbies of yours,
peace in your life is your slumber and snore,
dreams are the clouding that eases your score,
travels afar so you keep what you store.

Hobbies of mine can be hobbies of yours,
writing or reading is not at the store,
teaching yourself is the way to go far,
have enough gas if you must drive a car.

Hobbies of mine can be hobbies of yours,
take your degree and walk through abstract doors,
keep your ears open for unforeseen noise,
pressures of life have been changed to a toy.

Hobbies of mine can be hobbies of yours,
army fatigue can be khakis or shorts,
day turns to night then to blackness of dark,
all that will matter is that in your heart.

Painstakingly miserable

Facets of fallacies conveyed on human faces,
nothin' but trouble churning lubes of destruction-
facing hardship from economic tongue twisters
we all get duped, by heat seeking missiles
from inbred geeks guiding hell to city streets.

Reality

Reality crashes, wipes out the city
like a blind atom bomb,
striking through the wilderness
and clearing out the crops,
laughing like a human
pulling heists in front of cops.
Reality is neutral, its' arena undefined,
you know it when you see,
it lives in your eyes.
Pleasure or pain, depends on circumstance,
reality could bring a dollar or one hundred grand.
Could strip you of the things you have
or bring somethings to add,
anyway it's handled, reality won't care.
Anyway it's handled, reality won't care.

The land of OZ

(Serf to a quarter year of terrain)

The land of Oz begins when you start,
from sibling to woman,
feeding from light and dark.
Hidden from the virgin,
eye candy for the vet.
Rain brings vitamins,
sun makes my land smile,
care kills brown rust
on the edge of the child.

I asked August when
because she was first in line,
September breached our meet-
said October would be time.
A sign of frozen dew
is the clue for removal,
you can see the tee aeech
during change of venue.

Landing in Oz
the Yankees seem to be Chinese,
consumption is assimilation,
the natives have expertise.
Enter here, you won't leave and
by will you choose to seed.
A routine it shall be
to produce offspring,
fresh like new rain to
keep the corn children tamed.

Oz is Utopia and
its people are of nature,
the sun never sets
and warm weather is daily.
None dream of leaving,
few advertise their prize,
death is life sent without
deriving from demise.
Upon reaching Oz,

life changes through your *eyes*.

Snow

Winter weather is wild, the opposite child,
extreme at its worse and frigid at best.

Boldly sharpened air and steroid laced winds
freeze you on a limb as you breathe in.
Plains steeped in snow, streets ripe with ice,
sun leaves early as day turns to night.
Families grow closer, boy and girl cuddle,
eggs are fertilized, the act is not subtle.
Winter is cold and its flavor is bold,
taste of the season will never grow old.

Scarce Chance

Over a year ago arose the chance
to hopefully stake my claim in this life.
No reason for mistake lose once lose twice,
this woman at the stoplight was my wife.
No words were spoken she seemed out of sight,
the sole silhouette seen at the stoplight.

The story I told to a few was light,
embarrassed I am to bypass this chance
to chat with what at youth was in my sight,
no faculty involved, this is real life.
I could have met the queen to be my wife.
She was let go once but never will twice.

Wherever I may be I won't blink twice,
I know who I saw that day at that light;
a template of woman to call my wife.
At night sometimes I ask for a scarce chance
to dance with fears that occur in this life,
I'm anxious for her to show in my sight!

What appears to be gone will fall in sight,
I hope at least to say I saw her twice.
Again I may see it, that chance in life-
It's dark right now, someone can bring the light!
Surely often, I do think of the chance
to mix and chat, I should have made her wife!

God would only know if she was my wife,
she has the power to bring her in sight.
What right did I have to stupid the chance?

What to really do If I saw her twice?
Queen of all women seen at the stoplight,
if she has escaped I still love my life.

I value the good that happens in life,
just once have I claimed a stranger as wife.
A murder I committed of my light,
that day my ego was a flattened sight!
A pamper I need if she is seen twice,
my nerves will rise quicker at the next chance.

Learned Techniques

Eye to eye with black sheep who
do dirt on back street,
toe to toe with blue bloods who
do dirt on front street.
No love in this world,
no reason for uneven-
it's hard to move on when
loved ones are deceased.
Depending on the house
will make you lose a cow,
forgetting who you are inside
will make you die right now.
I view the world with tunnel
vision from inside my igloo,
learning ways to grow yourself
will make you learn yourself.
Dealing with these folk
enables you to stiffen,
working with the blue blood
could bring you to your sense.
Quarters, nickels
dimes and pennies,
all of which will spend,
may be the only currency
that makes it to the end.
Knowing of black sheep,
knowing of blue bloods
prepares you for the worse,
and the rain that's coming.

A new start

Mixing fire with water came out quite well,
a burst of energy flew out of a cell.
You'd think water would kill the fire,
the opposite happened, fire got stronger,
able to travel on top of the water,
sneaks in your room to bring in slaughter.

Mixing fire and water came out quite well,
the product itself would shorten your breath.
Scary it is to mix fire and water,
not for use by reason to martyr.
Our people debate, our people throw hate,
none of these people pave way to the gate.
Away from the hating away from debating,
out on my own to look for my own grapes.

Early mornings for me

On a very average day since 1998,
or before that,
I stayed immersed in vice
soon after I awoke.

On very average day since early in my age,
I wanted a world mended in my palm print.
I do quite well if I don't get sick,
at least to stay away from a blueprint.

On a strict hardy path
I crawl through mud,
no veterans give me hints
thoughts form naturally.

Endocrine Glands

Silence

Right now,
it's so quiet you can hear my eyes blink,
you can hear my blood flow,
you can hear my brain think.
Silence,
like this,
would kill the average man,
tame the wildest beast and
shell the drunkest fan.
I love my life but dislike myself,
I use dead silence to find who I am.

I really don't know

As I grew up I thought life was good,
in my young mind I knew this was wrong.

The world I knew was fun and fun games,
early in life I picked up on their game,
too young to comprehend, didn't know to play.
Mama's at work and she's bringin' in the bread,
never knew why she had to work a whole eight,
why I learned nothing from k until twelve,
or why I have not paved a path for myself.

As I think back I knew it was wrong,
I heard it ring, couldn't find the phone,
so with the normalcy I just went along.
My cognition deepened, I heard the phone ring,
found it,
picked it up-
and this is what I said:

"hello dear intruder,
I'm learning more and more,
your slumber and your snore
and utter hibernation
are ending as we speak,
prepare to end up faceless!"

Grandma's Heart

Grandma's heart surveys all
and never will I lie,
I look to her as monarch
until the day I die.
For those who used her
and claimed to play the part,
you'll be judged by God
and *also* Grandma's heart.

Scrap Metal

Pieces of a broken mirror
can be reassembled without glue,
love is the reinforcement
that remains shatterproof.
From minor to major
every story has an ending, almost
every broken heart can be mended.
Refuse to seek help
from psychiatric mystique,
make due with your brain
to end nights without sleep.
To fix the broken mirror
through years and tears,
one must thrust forward
in their own atmosphere.
Pieces of a broken mirror
can be reassembled without glue,
love is the reinforcement
that remains shatterproof.

It stuck with me

My mother told me everything,
everything she knew.
At an early age my vocabulary grew.
Half of what she said to me I never did forget,
mother said much, I can't remember everything-
then again I can,
the older that I get
I hear myself regurgitating everything she said.
Mothers' still here, hasn't went nowhere,
only feature different is the grey in her hair.

My word

If I don't have anything,
I have my word.
If I lose every dollar
I still have my word.

While the Euro grows and
home fiat weakens,
when you've been lied to,
I still have my word.

In a black panic war
I still have my word.
If the white house blew
I still have my word.

If you cry like
the boy who cried,
or you turn Pinocchio,
I still have my word.

In any year,
or when humans stop breathing,
if mammals lose hair
I still have my word.

Endocrine glands

Clashing with lions and tigers of hate,
the king of the jungle has taken the bait.
United we stand but divided at heart,
I pity the people who play in the dark.
A light is in light, the shadow will fear,
always take note of the power within.

No, thrice

Having a second father is never an option,
and no,
not referring to the in-law,
solely referring to he who calls shots,
watching what time you punch in the clock,
passing out checks you catch on that job
or tracking the places you go in your car.

Dos Padres? Oh no!
I choose to have one,
and no,
not one that sheds in the sun,
only the one that is full of melanin,
was in the trenches that I have been.

Here to help me never here to harm me,
a concrete fix in deep as a tree.
Not once, not twice,
to make a point I say thrice,
No no! No second father in my life!

¿Dónde?

Where can I find my jewelry?
Somewhere the truth is hidden.
I think I need to travel just
to see some different humans,
hidden worldly truths are
encrusted in the humans.

Where can I find my jewelry?
Bitch please, this ain't funny.
I really need it back
because you took it from me,
you placed it in your vault
and kept the secret from me.

Where can I find my jewelry?
Eventually,
I'll bite you
then ignite a world fire
instead of sitting silent.
This life is getting old
your visa has expired.

Where can I find my jewelry?
Eventually,
I'll find it...

You made it this far?

Thank you for your time and effort to support me in my artistic endeavors via poetry. Much love!

If at all you found any piece in this collection to be:

- ✓ Comical
- ✓ Decent to read
- ✓ Enjoyable
- ✓ Interesting
- ✓ Etc.,

please stay tuned in with me and on the lookout for the next volume in this collection:

Conversational Topography, Volume 2: *The Book of Macheté.*

I'm as anxious to release my next book as I was during the first book…I assure the content of the next book to be all original with its own explosive heartbeat of wordplay and imagery, if nothing else. See for yourself?

Your effort means much to an author who takes pride in their work. I personally thank anyone who laid eyes on my poetry and anyone that will. Thumbs up to ya!

Feedback!!!

Your feedback is pertinent. All feedback, whether positive or negative, is accepted.

Tell me: what you think, how you feel, if you don't feel, what you like or don't like, ideas, collaborations, requests, etc. SAY OR TYPE ANYTHING THAT YOU WOULD LIKE! I appreciate that concrete honesty. I don't care what it is, just say it.

Remember to:

Please maintain a humane level of professionalism when providing feedback. Be CORDIAL but speak your mind freely!

Direct *all* comments to:

Email: **DELANOCHEARTS@OUTLOOK.COM**

I look forward to hearing from YOU!

Special thanks to:

The following Channels:

The duke- You the man straight up. htp! We at the Beach!

Maddmike- Your readings are well put together, nice creativity.

Mr. Nightmare- Thanks to you I heard strange things in my house last spring……

Derek Murphy- You sparked my memory with Microsoft Word.

Awomansworld123- Prepping done the right way! Gon' head Mam.

To all channels listed above, I appreciate your works. When I was feeling down or in a study mode, especially in 2015, I came across a few pages while in random surf mode- you assisted me with entertainment and learning, or just random shits and giggles. I did not copy your ideas nor information*s*--but I do appreciate the time you put into your channel--believe me--I watch.

Questions??

1) Did you locate a poem to call your favorite?

2) Did you find a favorite line?

3) Have you ever thought of anything that you read in this collection, prior to reading it?

4) Did you read this collection more than once?

5) What do you think of the title of this collection?

6) Do you write poetry?

7) If I did a bad job at something, do you mind telling me exactly what that is?

8) Can you identify 3 of my favorite poems? If you can, I will write you a poem…you must identify at least 3.

9) Is there a poem you just don't agree with?

10) Where is my jewelry?

3———————

2—————————

1—————————

4———————

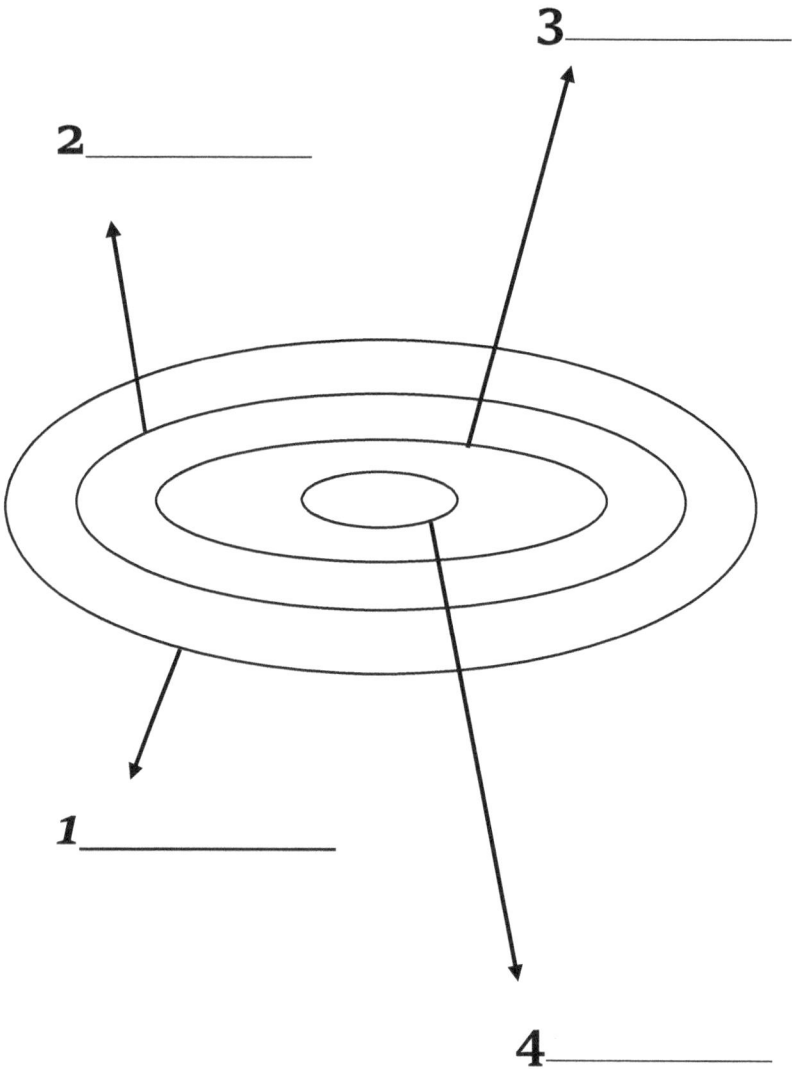

In your own ideas of <u>basic</u> topography, *fill in the blanks…*

110

Take this one with you…

(No title)

The same way you let me dry out in
the sun, freeze in the snow, get
caught in the rain, and blown away
in the wind is the same way you will
do me again…
so,
I'll pass…

Notes:

What's next?

Conversational Topography,

Volume 2:

The Book of Macheté

Please look out for it

Peace

Tres Amigos
de la noche

www.ingramcontent.com/pod-product-compliance
Lightning Source LLC
Chambersburg PA
CBHW020503030426
42337CB00011B/212